DON'T BE A COW!

FIND YOUR OWN PATH

A Collection of Daily Observations
and Lessons for Discovering
True Happiness!

by

George and Rachel Barker

LTU PUBLISHING
TALLASSEE, AL

George and Rachel Barker
LTU Publishing
PO Box 780172
Tallassee, AL 36078

Ordering Information:
Quantity sales. Special discounts are available on quantity purchases by corporations, associations, and others. For details, contact the "Special Sales Department" at the address above.

Don't Be A Cow/ George and Rachel Barker
ISBN 978-0692822180
1. Inspirational 2. Personal Growth 3. Self-Help 4. Journal
1st Edition

Illustrations and Cover design: Pat Achilles, achillesportfolio.com
Book Production and Editor: Gary S. James, jamesgang creative

Follow us on:
Facebook: Don't Be a Cow | Twitter: @dont_beacow | Instagram: dont_beacow

Dedication

First, we would like to dedicate this book to our characters A. Regular Joe and A. Plain Jane. Joe and Jane have allowed us to express a part of ourselves without exposing all of ourselves.

Second, we would like to thank all the regular Joes and Janes of this world who have touched our lives. This is everyone who has contributed to our life experiences without ever knowing it. It is these experiences we have chronicled in this book. No matter your societal status, we really are all regular Joes and Janes. Regular Joes and Janes trying to make sense of this thing we call life. It is but one journey that we all make; however, we all have our own individual path to blaze.

Third, our parents and family who helped create the foundation of who we are.

Fourth, but certainly not least, our four beautiful children: Thing 1, Thing 2, Thing 3 and Thing 4. They are the basis of our lives for the past 25 years. Unbeknownst to them, they kept us riding between the ditches more than they ever could realize and, of course, more than we would ever admit to.

Fifth, to all of those listed above who reinforced the saying, "Sometimes you have to laugh to keep from crying!" So, let's get laughing!

- George and Rachel

****

Employ your time in improving yourself
by other men's writings, so that you shall
gain easily what others have labored hard for.

- Socrates

Prologue

The dictionary defines "Happiness" as ...

Nope! This *ain't* that kind of book.

It all started one sunny spring day: No, no! It's not that kind of book either!

As you might have guessed from the title, this book is a little different than most. We hope you enjoy different.

"Don't Be A Cow" is a fun metaphor to remind us to be the person we are meant to be. (Note the picture above: The cows have an entire pasture in which to roam yet they choose to follow each other in single file.) If we are not careful as we walk through life, we too, will act like cows, following the path of others instead of blazing our own path.

Don't Be A Cow!

Okay, so what does this have to do with happiness you might ask? Living a life of happiness centers on finding and staying true to your own unique path, and only you can find your path.

> "No one saves us but ourselves,
> No one can and no one may,
> We ourselves must walk the path."
> - Buddha

Today it seems that so many are in search of happiness.

> "We all desire to be happy."
> - Dalai Lama

Although many seek, many cannot find because they are looking for the wrong thing. Happiness is a life style, a way of life, and not simply a feeling or a mood. True happiness is about living a fulfilling and peaceful life in all that you do. Will you also experience other emotions such as sorrow and frustration while living this "happy life"? Absolutely! Happiness will create a feeling of inner peace, a sort of a warm and fuzzy feeling within. A feeling you will want to share with others and you will share it because it will radiate from you in all that you do.

Book Layout

Although the book is laid out in 31 Daily reminders, there are no instructions. If you wish to read it all at once, you certainly won't perish! Each Daily reminder includes the following:

- Picture and supporting dialogue between Joe and Jane; we used dialog because we felt our points could be made using fewer words. We believe in brevity.

- Soulful note - No matter your religious preference those who have walked before us provide great insight and perspective into daily living. Some are from religious leaders, others are not.

- Song - What better expression of happiness then wanting to get up and dance? Music can help us reach our inner selves in an unbelievable way.

  "Music washes away from the soul the dust of everyday life."
  - Berhold Auerbach

Note: Music is a personal choice and moves us all differently. The songs chosen for this book are songs that appeal to Joe and Jane, and they tried to cross genre and generations. You are encouraged to make your own playlist as you move through each day, and play it often to remind yourself, through song, your path to happiness. Joe and Jane's complete playlist is provided in the back of the book, along with blank play list sheet for you to create your own.

We also provide:

- Game Exercises - Meant to be fun, and to help make each daily reminder a part of your everyday life. A cheat sheet is provided in the back of the book. The cheat sheet is provided for you to write a few of the game exercise responses that you find most useful. When you have finished the book, tear out the cheat sheet and keep it where you can access it quickly.

Each day is meant to stand on its own merit; however, the book does build upon itself in helping you discover your path.

Meet Joe and Jane:

Joe and Jane have two philosophies employed in this book:

- Brevity is the soul of wisdom.

- Simplicity can be found in complexity.

They are not doctors, nor have PhD's. He is a regular Joe, she's a plain Jane. They have no formal training in psychology, psychiatry or any other studies of the human brain. They do believe we all become somewhat brain docs simply going through life interacting with other humans, especially in the fine art of raising children! Basically, they are, well, regular people. Maybe a tad bit more observant than others! Enough from us; let's hear a quick word from Joe and Jane:

Joe: This book has been a great <u>adventure</u> and although I have been the main instigator, I could have never accomplished it without Jane.

Jane: It has been fun, and I think what has made it so much fun is it's a book about living. It's not an instruction manual but a composite of living our lives and learning what others have said in regards to their lives.

Joe: So true, Jane. I feel like I "lived" the book and didn't "write" the book.

Joe & Jane:

Good luck, enjoy and feel free to make your own contribution of things you have used to make your life happier! And always remember to find your path, and...

Don't Be A Cow!

Terminology:

There are certain words or phrases that are used in this book that can help provide guidance in your <u>quest</u> to find happiness. Whenever you see a word underlined, you'll find it on this page.

<u>Adventure</u> - Go on one everyday!!!

<u>Challenge (ing)</u> - Always use as a substitute for hard or difficult.

<u>Cowism</u> - The act of being like everyone else.

<u>Expectations</u> - The understanding that perception can in fact be realities!

<u>Extraordinary</u> - Make your life. Whoever sets out to be ordinary - Boring!

<u>Influence</u> - Far better than control. It relies on action, not words! Ouch!

<u>Quest</u> - A nice word that speaks to the journey not the destination.

<u>Seek</u> - To look for with purpose and with no end.

<u>Whos</u> - The fine people in the Christmas classic, *The Grinch who Stole Christmas*. Everything taken except their souls! What a story!

<u>Zest</u> - Get up and go; this is a fun and refreshing word.

Used together:

I wake each morning with <u>zest</u>, knowing not where the day will lead; but, I know it's certain to be an <u>adventure</u>, as I continue my <u>quest</u> to discover my path (talents) and thereby making my life <u>extraordinary</u>. I also have the <u>expectations</u> that all my thoughts can become reality, which gives me purpose, that I may have an <u>influence</u> on others, which may make a positive difference in the world. I also acknowledge that there are many in this walk through life who will entice me towards <u>cowism</u>. This effort will be made up of family, friends and strangers alike. Many of the attempts to turn me to <u>cowism</u> will be honest attempts to help me. They will have "my best interest at heart." Although many of these intentions will be for "my best interest," I understand that I must continually <u>seek</u> my path (my gift to the world) yielding me the happiness I deserve. Understanding at times this will be a <u>challenging</u> task, but I will arise to the <u>challenge</u>! If the <u>Whos</u> can do it after losing everything, then so can I!

This is Happiness!

Soulful Enhancement & Song

Soulful:

"Great works are performed not by strength but by perseverance."

- Samuel Jackson

Song:

"Life is a Highway"
- Rascal Flatts

This song seems to say it all in just a few words. Life is like an endless highway, the scenery will change, some pretty, some not so, the pavement will change, some smooth some bumpy, the weather the sky will all change your only choice is which direction and whether or not you are coming or going! The song is also full of energy (which we need to ride this highway of life).

Prologue

List at least 5 - 10 words and/or phrases that you like. Ones that make you feel good. Remember this book is all about you.

D A Y 1

Be Who You Are!

Joe: Do you see any resemblance to our book cover, Jane?

Jane: I sure do! Scary!!!

Joe: For reasons that I don't understand, we humans choose to imitate cows. With all kinds of options in life and limitless numbers of paths to choose, we tend to follow the ones everyone else chooses!

Robert Frost describes it this way:

> "Two roads diverged in a wood and I - I took the one less traveled by, and that has made all the difference."

Jane: Yeah! Family, friends and society (people we don't even know!) try to dictate the paths we walk.

Joe: And often with good intentions, I might add.

Jane: These worn and established paths are certainly comfortable and can lead to comfortable places.

Joe: Yeah, the paths the cows follow do generally lead to the food trough and the watering hole.

Jane: So the real question becomes, is that all you are looking for in life?

Joe: Or is there more?

> "There are two ways to slice easily through life -- to believe everything or to doubt everything. Both ways save us from thinking."
> - Alfred Korzybski

Jane: And this, my friends, is what it's all about. Think about the adventures awaiting you by simply getting out of line, moving out of the well worn path walked by so many and finding your own path, finding you.

YOUR PATH: In order to find happiness, you must first find your path, your talent to share with the world. When you are on your path you will find it easier staying true to your path.

Don't Be A Cow!

Be you.

Soulful Enhancement & Song

Soulful:

> "For the one body does not consist of one member but many.... If
> the whole body were an eye, where would be the hearing... On
> the contrary, the parts of the body which seem to be weaker are
> indispensable ... And God has appointed in the church first
> apostles, second prophets ... helpers, administrators ..."
> - I Corinthians 12:14, 17,22, 28

We can't all be eyes, ears, or noses, just as we can't all be rock stars, doctors or professional athletes. No matter what we are, we are all indispensable. You may think your eyes are more important than your nose, until it is the nose that smells the smoke, while you and your family sleep, which awakens you and allows you to get all out unscathed. Never underestimate the significance of your talent.

Song:

> "Stand In The Light"
> - Jordan Smith

The song makes reference to that fact that when we put ourselves out in the open as our "true self" we take a huge risk, but remember the rewards are just as huge! What is that reward? Happiness!

Song (A tie today):

> "Try"
> - Colbie Cailat

Although the song is aimed at young girls, it applies to all and has a fun beat!

D A Y 1

Be Who You Are!

GAME EXERCISE

Identify times and situations where you have noticed humans imitating Cows! MOOO!

Place a check mark by the ones you fell in line with too?

Identify times, situations, or people who have made or tried to make you be a Cow!

Write in very large print the following:

I Will

<u>Not</u>

Be

A Cow.

<u>D A Y 2</u>

Learn to Smile

Joe: Smiling makes you feel good.

Jane: Yes it does and every time you feel good, I bet you're smiling.

Joe: Indeed it works in reverse too.

Jane: Smiling seems so simple. I mean, unless you are having one of those days.

Joe: You would be surprised, Jane! Have you ever noticed facial expressions when you are in a public place or even within your own household for that matter?

Jane: Yeah, I suppose you're right. There's not a lot of smiling going on out there!

Joe: The next time you are out and about, look around at the people who you would consider attractive, just don't look too close! I am willing to bet that they are all smiling!

Jane: You are right about that. When I make a conscious effort to smile, I've noticed that I get more compliments on my clothes and my hairstyle and I've changed neither. Sort of bizarre if you ask me.

Joe: It can actually be quite fun.

Jane   Absolutely, especially when you get compliments on your clothes and hairstyle!

Joe: Smiling will almost immediately make you feel better within. And, when people compliment you or simply acknowledge you with a "Good Morning" or "Hello" - which they are more likely to do if you are smiling - you immediately feel better about yourself.

Jane: And the one thing you need, as you <u>seek</u> your path, is to feel good about who you are. It can all start with a smile.

YOUR PATH: When you feel better about yourself you are less likely to leave your path for the comfort of another's thus helping you to stay true to your path.

Have you ever seen a cow smile?

Don't Be A Cow!

Soulful Enhancement & Song

Soulful:

> "We shall never know all the good that a simple smile can do."
> – Mother Teresa

Song:

> "Smile"
>
> - Nat King Cole

The song addresses the importance of smiling even when times are tough. It can really be a game changer.

D A Y 2

Learn to Smile

GAME EXERCISE

How to Smile

Put your face about ten inches in front of a mirror. Look yourself right in the eye and say the word "great" in as many different ways as you can: angry, loud, soft, sexy, like Jerry Lewis ... Keep going. Eventually you'll crack up. Repeat the exercise once a day for three days. The next time you meet someone say "great" under your breath three times and you'll be smiling. [1]

Joe: Personally, I like practicing different smiles in front of the mirror. I try to create a different smile for every occasion. But, it does require practice, and generally gets me laughing.

Jane: You can always manage to crack yourself up ... a natural ham! However, for the rest of us, the key is to discover what works best for you. The real test is to go out into the world (work, store, doctor's office, church) smiling, write your experiences below.

---

[1] Nicholas Boothman, *Convince Them in 90 Seconds* (New York, NY: Workman Publishing, 2010).

D A Y 3

Learn to Laugh

Joe: Yesterday we started smiling into the mirror.

Jane: So I assume today you are going to say that we need to make ourselves laugh in the mirror?

Joe: That's right; after all, smiling is simply step one to laughing. See how funny you can get your own face in the mirror!

Jane: Can't we try something other than the mirror?

Joe: Certainly. Try recalling a funny moment in your life or a good joke; however, the good thing about making yourself laugh in the mirror is that you can see yourself laugh at yourself. Today people often seem to be too uptight, too serious. Much of this comes from the *cow syndrome*; we can only laugh when the lead cow laughs.

Jane: You're right. In fact, it was Ethel Barrymore who once said,

> "You grow up the day you have the first real
> laugh at yourself."

Joe: See, it's not just me making this stuff up!

Jane: I know there have been countless studies on laughter and its positive effects on our health and our daily lives.

Joe: Yeah, there is research on everything these days, but laughter is one of those things that we have all experienced its positive effects. It just makes us feel good.

Jane: And think about it, have you ever seen a cow laugh?

YOUR PATH: When you can laugh at yourself, what could others ever do to you that would prevent you from staying true to your path?

Don't Be A Cow!

Laugh.

Soulful Enhancement & Song

Soulful:

"If I had no sense of humor, I would long ago have committed suicide."

- Mahatma Gandhi

Song:

"The Mississippi Squirrel Revival"

- Ray Stevens

This is a good opportunity to inject that what some find funny others do not. It is all dependent on our own individual life experiences. For this laughing can certainly point to <u>cowism</u> when we laugh because everyone else does or even worse when we think something is funny yet no one else is laughing so we suppress our own laughter. Granted sometimes it is the polite thing to do, but be careful it's not because of the company we are in.

DAY 3

Learn to Laugh

GAME EXERCISE

Below, write down times in your life that were really funny. In some cases you may not even remember all the specifics, but you remember laughing hysterically.

Put an asterisk by any that involve laughing at yourself or makes fun of a personal quirk that you may have. Now keep these where you can access them when you need a good laugh.

Jane: I made a folder I keep in my desk that I clip out funny jokes and pictures. When the folder gets too thick, I recycle out old ones. What's funny is to see people walk into my office shortly after I have looked through the folder.

Joe: This one will add <u>zest</u> to your life and make it <u>extraordinary</u>!

D A Y 4

"Want to"

Do you want to be happy?

Do you want to have a fulfilling life?

Do you want to enjoy life?

Do you want to bring good things to others?

Do you want to be successful?

Joe: Have you ever seen such determination?

Jane: I'm saying! But, isn't having "want to" a given? I mean everyone wants to.

Joe: You're right or it seems so anyway; however, things happen that derail us. Those things are both internal and external <u>influences.</u> It is the combination of both which can lead us to <u>cowism.</u>

Jane: Explain that one!

Joe: First internal: we must examine our inner most self and ask ourselves the question, do I have the "want to," to live my life, without fear of failure, without fear of being laughed at, or ridiculed? The "want to," to be who I am!

Jane: Okay, I can understand that. What about the external?

Joe: Your teachers, parents, friends, and society as a whole. Others defining your "want to." These are based on job security, societal norms (what's popular today), family traditions, or any number of things. In any event, they are the paths made for you by others.

Jane: I'm sure this scenario is played out over and over again in life. But, why?

Joe: Mostly with good intentions, but others base your "want to" on their own experiences and their perceptions of your talents and not *your* "want to."

Jane: Yeah, that's right. Like, if you're great at math, everyone thinks you should be an engineer.

Joe: That's right, and unfortunately, it can start at a very young age. This can lead us to believing it as well.

Jane: I get it! So, if we were lead to believe it, we may have never stopped to think, is this my "want to"?

Joe: Yes, and it is often so subtle that we don't even realize it or if we do realize it, it is just easier to put on our cow uniform and follow the path laid by others.

Jane: How do we avoid falling into that trap?

Joe: Keep reading this book!

YOUR PATH: Remember even the paths the cows follow lead to the watering hole, which isn't such a bad place, but is it your place? Examine *your* "want to," and take the first step to making your life _extraordinary_! It will lead you to a path you never knew existed and once on your path you will have little trouble staying true to your path!

Don't Be A Cow!

Discover your "want to"
and live your life extraordinary.

Soulful Enlightenment & Song

Soulful:

> "We choose our joys and sorrows long before we experience them."
>
> > - Kahlil Gibran

We choose (we need to have "want to") if we want to enjoy the life we have.

Song:

> "Don't Stop Believin'"
>
> > - Journey

This is a nice upbeat song about two young people leaving home in a quest to find their "want to." You see, sometimes you have to do more than sit around and think about your "want to."

DAY 4

"Want to"

GAME EXERCISE

To have "want to" everyday, requires motivation. We go through times when "want to" comes naturally and other times when we have to really work at it.

Think of what has motivated you in the past, maybe a song that really gets you fired up, a movie, or a news story about someone over coming great odds. Write some of these below, then put some of them in a readily accessible place (Your cheat sheet in the back of book). These will serve as little reminders for those days when you just seem to be having a hard time with "want to."

DAY 5

Discipline

Practice the Art

Joe: You know, Jane, people often think of discipline as real hard and real ridged like the military, but it doesn't have to be.

Jane: Yeah, people practice discipline everyday and just don't realize it. I mean things such as getting out of bed, removing make up, and brushing teeth, for example.

Joe: William Feather once wrote, "If we do not discipline ourselves the world will do it for us."

Jane: Um, maybe that's why so many of us get turned into cows. Because that's what happens when the world disciplines us: Don't Be A Cow!

Joe: Developing a disciplined life style doesn't have to be difficult, nor rigid, but it is so very important.

Jane: Yeah, it will be a major building block to your success.

Joe: I once heard someone say, "that you should get up every morning and make your bed first thing. This way no matter what happens that day you will have already accomplished one thing."

Jane: That's an excellent example of practicing the Art of Discipline.

Joe: Discipline is so important. It gives us confidence in ourselves, i.e. helps us believe in ourselves, and our abilities to accomplish things.

Jane: It is the one thing that allows us to control our own lives.

Joe: And it can really be sort of fun to practice.

YOUR PATH: Discipline is key to finding and remaining on your path. There will always be plenty of others trying to get you to join them and follow on their path; however, discipline will allow you to stay true to your path.

Don't Be A Cow!

<u>Seek</u> discipline. Control you.

Soulful Enhancement and Song

Soulful:

"For the moment all discipline seems painful rather than pleasant, later it yields the peaceful fruit of righteousness to those who have been trained by it."

- Hebrews 12:11

The author talks about training for discipline, not running a marathon or some other task, but he refers to training for discipline for disciplines sake. Please don't under estimate the importance of this concept.

Song:

"Gonna Fly Now"

- Bill Conti, theme song from *Rocky*, the motion picture

Although this is not specifically about discipline, Rocky certainly practiced discipline in the strictest sense of the word and is inspiring.

D A Y   5

Discipline

GAME EXERCISE

This is one that you need to put some thought into. It is really a springboard for everything else that follows. Below, write down some things that you already do every day.

Now, write down one you can add. Remember start small. Here are some ideas:

- Drink a small glass of water every night before you go to bed or first thing every morning or both.

- Do one push-up every night before going to bed (don't allow yourself to do two).

- Making a funny face in the mirror every morning.

- Have a mini-candy bar after every lunch and supper. This is fun and yummy, but not as easy as it may sound - to make sure you always have one with you.

Remember this is not exercise time, cleaning time or a time to make yourself miserable, but a time to practice the Art of Discipline. Once you have mastered one small task, try adding a new one, maybe one more challenging.

DAY 6

Take Time for You

Remember Who **You** Are!

(A great line from *The Lion King*)

Jane: Sometimes, in order to be selfless, you must first be selfish.

Joe: Flight attendants, during pre flight safety, instruct you to put on your own oxygen mask before helping others. For a parent with a small child this would not be as easy as it sounds. The concept is simple: How can you take care of someone else, if you can't take care of yourself?

Jane: This can be especially difficult for mothers!

Joe: Yet as the flight attendant instructs, if the mother were to run out of oxygen while trying to help her child, both could end up in trouble.

Jane: And, I think we all understand that, but so often we get caught up in day-to-day life we ignore ourselves.

Joe: Yes, we are trying to put everyone else's mask on, and we are the ones who end up running out of oxygen.

Jane: Like with the oxygen mask, a mother who spends a few minutes with herself everyday can provide so much more for her family.

Joe: Exactly, so why not take a few minutes every day and breath in a little oxygen? *(Take time for you).*

Jane: This is the only way; I mean the *only* way you can ever find your path, your gift to share with the world.

Joe: You know, Jane, the oxygen analogy is really a good one because we all know, without oxygen, we will fail to exist, and when we don't make time for ourselves, we won't exist (as our true self) either. We will simply succumb to cowism by following the lead of others. Moooo!

YOUR PATH: Take time for you, remember who you are! This is ever so hard today with 24/7 television, cell phones and social media; however, it is the only way you will ever discover and stay true to your path.

Don't Be A Cow!

Take time for you.

Soulful Enhancement and Song

Soulful:

"...We discovered that sitting down just to think is one of the best ways of keeping yourself fresh and able, to be able to address the problems facing you."

-Nelson Mandela

"Faith is an oasis in the heart which can never be reached by the caravan of thinking."

- Kahlil Gibran

The "caravan of thinking" is where others will choose your path for you!

Song: (A Tie Today)

"Lord is it Mine"

- Supertramp

The song refers to a silent place that brings peace and tranquility from the worries of the world. The place is so special they question if it is actually theirs.

"In My Room"

-The Beach Boys

This one a little more direct and to the point but conveys the importance of having a place to go to spend time with you.

D A Y 6

Take Time for You

GAME EXERCISE

List some places and times you could find time for yourself, and that don't involve multi-tasking: 5 minutes a day … 30 is better. Some ideas:

- Driving without the phone or radio on.

- Sitting in the back yard listening to the wind.

- Take a walk or hike.

- Take a soothing bath or shower.

DAY 7

Nature

The Vastness! The Splendor!

The Beauty!

The Complexity! The Simplicity!

WOW!

Joe: Need we say anything more? A picture really is worth a thousand words.

Jane: Uh, well, yeah! With all the modern conveniences (and inconveniences), we often lose sight of the simple - and free I might add - things in life.

Joe: It's that feeling of being a part of something yet a feeling of being so inconsequential.

Jane: Experiencing nature is an experience that some really connect with, but whether you connect or not, it can be soothing to the soul and relaxing to the mind and body.

Joe: It can be quite simple and fun and certainly offers numerous opportunities for adventure!

Jane: You know, combining Days 6 & 7 can really provide an over-the - top experience that can be life changing.

Joe: A quest to explore and discover something new.

YOUR PATH: Observing and being a part of nature will help you understand and appreciate your own uniqueness. Knowing and understanding your uniqueness will enable you to stay true to your path.

Don't Be A Cow!

Add the zest of nature to your life.

Soulful Enhancement and Song

Soulful:

"He knew that man's heart, away from nature, becomes hard."

- Luther Standing Bear, Oglala Sioux chief

Song:

"What A Wonderful World"

- Louis Armstrong

DAY 7

Nature

GAME EXERCISE

- Buy an outdoor rocking chair hammock or swing.

- Put up a humming bird feeder or bird feeder.

- Take a hike in a park.

- Stand in the rain (preferably, without lightning!).

To force yourself to observe your surroundings, write down below what you saw and what you thought! Have fun, do what you want and with whom you want, just do it outside and notice what is going on around you. Be amazed.

DAY 8

Be Positive

Joe: This truly is a state of mind.

Jane: Explain ...

Joe: Think about the last time you woke in the morning to do something you really wanted to do. Did you have to hit the snooze button several times?

Jane: No, not at all. I was up, showered and ready to go in half the time it normally takes.

Joe: Exactly, so why don't you wake like this every day?

Jane: Because, this was going to be special day. I was doing something I really wanted to do!

Joe: My first response to that would be, why don't you do what you want every day? So in other words, you think it's going to be a great day ... maybe even a perfect day?

Jane: Exactly! And, I didn't just think it. I knew it.

Joe: But can't bad things happen, even happen on these days? I mean, flat tires, delayed airplanes, lost luggage, your dog dies ...

Jane: ... I guess so, but who ever worries about that on a special day!

Joe: Exactly my point. Then the only real difference between a regular day and a special day is our <u>expectations</u> of the day that lays in wait! And certainly, you understand that <u>expectations</u> are all in our heads. They have no relationship to what actually may transpire that day.

Jane: Interesting. I never thought of it in that way.

Joe: The really great thing is, once we recognize that it is all in our head, we can capitalize on the power that comes with it.

Jane: Power?

Joe: Yes Power, in the form of energy. Think about the energy you had when you woke on that special day.

Jane: Oh, I had energy all right! I was bouncing from one room to the next, like a five-year-old on Christmas morning!

Joe: Never forget the power and energy created from positive thinking.

YOUR PATH: Once you understand the power and energy associated with positive thinking, you will <u>seek</u> to make it a part of your everyday life; thus providing you the energy to find and stay true to your path.

Don't Be A Cow!
Be positive.

Soulful Enhancement and Song

Being positive really means believing in yourself and having faith in your abilities. When you believe in yourself you understand that you are going to make mistakes you understand that others may even laugh at you or talk about you behind your back but you know in the end you will prevail. Christ is validating this concept; you have to believe. Imagine addressing Jesus with "if you can."

Soulful:

> "... if you can, do anything, have pity on us and help us." And Jesus said to him, "If you can! All things are possible to him who believes."
>
> - Mark 9:22-23

Song:

> "The Devil Went Down to Georgia"
>
> - The Charlie Daniels Band

This is a fun song where a man's belief in himself is on full display. The fiddle player is so positive in his abilities as a fiddle player he bets his soul against the devil.

D A Y 8

Be Positive

GAME EXERCISE

In today's exercise we want to emphasis and reinforce the concept:

> *People who believe in themselves are Positive People and*
> *Positive People believe in themselves.*

Write down several times when you can remember bouncing out of bed with great <u>expectations</u> for that day: Remember the excitement, the energy!

Write down several times when you believed in yourself when you really felt confident. Note the same energy as above. You may want to transfer one or two of these to your cheat sheet in the back of the book.

DAY 9

Squash Negative Thoughts

Joe: "No Date for the Prom," "Wrecked the Car," "Cut from the Team," "Your Fired!" Man, some of these negative thoughts can really occupy your mind.

Jane: Yes, they can, and that is why it is so important to get them out of your head.

Joe: And replace them with positive ones, I might add! This way our mind remains engaged and is less likely to drift back to another negative thought.

Jane: Yeah, but no matter how hard we try sometimes, these negative or unwanted thoughts just seem to keep popping into our heads and then act as weights tied to our ankles as we go through the day trying to be positive.

Joe: Yes, and this is the exact reason I put positive before negative. We must always remember that positive thoughts create energy and negative thoughts do just the opposite. As you described they feel like weights tied around your ankles.

Jane: Okay, so I guess this is an important concept.

Joe: Yes, it is! Image the follow scenario: You're sitting in a lobby outside a conference room waiting for your interview. As you patiently wait, this thought continues to run through your head, "they aren't going to like me, I just know it," over and over again. Then you replace it with "they liked me on the phone interview and granted me this opportunity, they are going to love me!" Then, the smile begins to spread across your face.

Jane: That's it: Squash, replace and smile. If you are finding it hard to squash, try applying a little discipline and force a small smile. You will find that the "replace" becomes easier.

Joe: That's nice, a little Day 2 and Day 5 thrown in there. This stuff really does build on itself. I like to think of it as running an obstacle course. Each time a negative thought occurs, it's like a new obstacle to overcome. The obstacles are a test to see just how bad we want the things we want.

Jane: One thing is certain, negative thoughts will keep us from being who we are meant to be, keeping us from reaching our full potential. They keep us in Cow Town!

Joe: There may be days where it seems like they keep coming at you. Just remember Squash, replace and smile, in the end you will prevail.

Jane: You have a gift, come share it with the rest of us.

YOUR PATH: Negative thoughts will take you off your path every time because they allow doubt to enter. You must practice discipline to "Squash" them every time they pop into your head. Thus, you will find it easier to stay true to your path.

Don't Be A Cow!

Use squash.

Soulful Enhancement and Song

Soulful:

> "It takes but one positive thought when given a chance to survive and thrive to overpower an entire army of negative thoughts."
>
> - Robert H. Schuller

Song:

> "X's and O's"
>
> - Elle King

Even though this song is referring to past loves, which are negatives thoughts in their own right, it could be negative thoughts of all types. This song describes exactly how they can haunt us!

DAY 9

Squash Negative (Unwanted) Thoughts

GAME EXERCISE

Below, write a few times you were constantly plagued with negative thoughts running through your head:

Next to each place an (E), external (caused by others being critical), or an (I), internal (caused from your own self doubt). Of the ones with an (I), underline the ones that were caused by a foolish or thoughtless act that you performed and circle the ones that were just negative thoughts that question our own abilities. Visualize shaking these thoughts out of your head (*maybe out your ear*) and landing on the ground. Squash them with you foot!

DAY 10

What Do You Want?

Joe: No, this isn't what I'm looking for!

Jane: Then, Joe, what exactly are you looking for? I mean, it's mighty difficult to find something if you don't know what it is.

Joe: That is true. Isn't it amazing how many people cannot answer this seemingly simple question?

Jane: Yes it is. This is a question you should be able to answer the instant someone asks it. I mean, this should be the reason you get out of bed every day.

Joe: And, when you know what it is it will add <u>zest</u> to your life for sure.

Jane: Then why do you think so many people can't?

Joe: That is both an interesting and difficult question to tackle, and I'm sure it varies greatly, but I do have a theory.

Jane: Like that's a big surprise! So, what's your theory?

Joe: When we are young children we are so full of life and so full of dreams, which I might add, contributes to the energy of young tikes. We never question if these dreams are realistic. Without the "realism" component, we wake every morning believing all our dreams (or thoughts) will come to be. (Note that dreams and thoughts are used synonymously.) As we get older, realism enters and the two become very separate. Along with realism comes negativism introduced by outside influences - Cows, I might add.

Jane: It's sort of like dreams become what we want while our thoughts are more concerned with our needs.

Joe: That is a great way to describe it! And, over time we become so preoccupied with our needs we forget all about our wants.

Jane: If we *do* think of our wants we classify them as dreams: Dreams that are unattainable, nothing more than happy thoughts.

Joe: Exactly right!

Jane: To make matters worse this conversion to "realism" generally develops during the teen years.

Joe: That's right, those brain-dead teen years when the growth of the body greatly outpaces the growth of the mind and soul.

Jane: And when outside influences are the greatest I might add.

Joe: Absolutely, this is why we have to re-program ourselves. We have to look at what we really want out of life and then change our wants to needs. Needs that we feel we must obtain to live a fulfilling life.

YOUR PATH: In order to live a happy, fulfilling life you must define exactly what it is that will provide it for you! When, and only when, you know "What you Want" will you be able to stay true to your path.

Don't Be A Cow!

Know exactly what you are looking for.

Soulful Enhancement and Song

Soulful:

> "When you ask, you do not receive, because you ask with wrong motive, that you may spend what you get on your pleasures."
>
> - James 4: 3

When our motives are pure, our desires will be met.

Song:

> "You Can't Always Get What You Want"
>
> -The Rolling Stones

… But, if you try sometimes you may just find you get what you need. Admittedly, an unlikely pairing James and Jagger; however they are, in essence, saying the same thing. Our needs are produced from our true self (i.e. correct motives); whereas, our wants are produced from societal pressures, (i.e. wrong motives). The truth lies in understanding deep down inside, what do you want? because for each of us, this is what you need.

DAY 10

What Do You Want?

GAME EXERCISE

Below, write down: What it is you want? Allow the energy to consume you.

Suggestion: Start in general terms and then begin to add the specifics (this could take additional paper, but that's great).

For Example: You want a new career: Don't just write down the new type of job you want, but write down the hours, the type of office (or work place), the commute distance, the type of clothes and travel; or if a new house is what you want, draw a floor plan and find pictures of the exterior you like. Spare nothing. And, have fun!

D A Y 1 1

Visualize

Joe: Ouch! It looks like he is making things harder than they actually are.

Jane: I would say he has a thought that needs squashing!

Joe: Great athletes describe visualization as vital. You will see golfers stand behind the ball before they hit visualizing the shot they are trying to hit. Great basketball players visualize the ball going through the hoop as they shoot.

Jane: They say if a skier looks down as opposed to looking forward, they are sure to fall.

Joe: You will go where your eyes carry you, that is for sure.

Jane: So why not see a good ending and instead of a bad?

Joe: Yesterday we defined what it is we want. Today, we need to visualize being what we want. Just as the golfer visualizes the shot he wants, you must visualize you being what it is you want.

Jane: It can be difficult because we become skeptical. We begin to believe that good things can't happen to us.

Joe: Just like the picture indicates, it can be so difficult to get rid of those unwanted images.

Jane: But I also think that sometimes it is the result of not having a clear idea of what it is you want.

Joe: By knowing what you want and visualizing it (positive image) you become better able to squash the negative image that will always try to surface.

Jane: But without knowing what it is you want, you simply have random images so the negative images, which are not so random will always prevail.

Joe: The golfer, when distracted while standing over the ball, stops - walks back behind the ball and visualizes the shot he wants once more. The distraction made him lose the vision of the shot he wanted. Like golf, life will give us many opportunities to lose our vision of who we want to be.

Jane: We must always be willing (Day 4: Want To and Day 5: Discipline) to stop, refocus and form the image of *who* it is we want to be.

YOUR PATH: Visualize what it is you want and then you can overcome negativism and stay true to your path!

Don't Be A Cow!
Visualize who you want to be.

Soulful Enlightenment and Song

Soulful:

"I never hit a shot, not even in practice, without having a very sharp, in-focus picture of it in my head."

- Jack Nicklaus

"Visualization is the most powerful thing we have."

- Nick Faldo

Two of the greatest golfers of all time describe the importance of visualizing. Visualize what you want, and then make it happen.

Remember dreams are simply what you really want!

Song:

"Paint Me A Birmingham"

- Tracy Lawrence

One thing is for certain: He certainly has a clear vision of what he wants as he asked the painter to paint himself back into his girlfriends arms again!

DAY 11

Visualize

GAME EXERCISE

Today's game requires no writing just reflecting. Look at the list you made yesterday. Close your eyes and see that person going to work or see that person in the new house. Think detail: What kind of clothes, car, friends, co-workers, swagger and attitude, etc. Keep your eyes closed until this image is firmly implanted. (Repeat daily).

Suggestion: Sometimes we become so entrenched in our thoughts that we forget to smile even though we are having the time of our life. Don't forget this all-important ingredient. It will have an impact on your vision. Trust us.

<u>D A Y 1 2</u>

Revisit #3: Learn to Laugh

Joe: You know, Jane, you can never learn this lesson enough.

Jane: Especially you, Joe. You have to laugh to keep from crying most of the time!

Joe: Very funny!

Joe: All kidding aside, sometimes life can start moving really fast.

Jane: You can say that again …

Joe: Sometimes life can start moving really fast.

Jane: Ha-ha, well it is learn-to-laugh day.

Joe: It is always a good idea to slow ourselves down and reflect.

Jane: Are you suggesting we all do that today?

Joe: I am. We are nearing the halfway point and some of us are probably feeling pretty good about our progress, some are probably scratching their heads in bewilderment, and some are probably still trying to soak it all in.

Jane: Yeah, like, "I got this!"

Joe: Exactly, so before we start our climb to the finish line, let's take a quick look back to day three.

Jane: I understand, but Day 3 ... Really?

Joe: Yeah, really. We always need to remind ourselves to laugh, especially at ourselves. Lighten up. Chill out. Let's not take things too seriously.

Jane: You know, you are probably the only person alive that would put laughing twice.

Joe: Yes, but I didn't put it until Day 3 the first time. Yes, I do think it is that important! Often when we think of laughter, we think of jokes, but they say we actually laugh more about life situations than we do at jokes.

Jane: Honestly, just walk down a sidewalk or sit on a bench where people are. It generally doesn't take long. Often you do find yourself laughing to keep from crying! Boy, does it add <u>zest </u>to life.

Joe: When you can laugh at yourself, you begin to remove some of the inner walls that keep yourself from finding *you.*

Jane: It's sort of like when we laugh at ourselves, we are saying, I'm okay with me, with who I am.

YOUR PATH: Use laughter to help tear down the inner walls, revealing you, and then you will find the going easier to stay true to your path.

Don't Be A Cow!

Laugh.

$\Big($Ever see a cow laugh?$\Big)$

Soulful Enlightenment and Song

Soulful:

"If we weren't all crazy we would go insane."

- Jimmy Buffet

Song:

"Lonestar"

- Mr. Mom

This song may actually hit too close to home to the parents and baby sitters out there! Always remember that the happenings of life always provide the best humor and don't forget to laugh at yourself.

DAY 12

Revisit Day 3: Learn to Laugh

GAME EXERCISE

Revisit your list from Day 3, and enjoy the laugh, or add to it below. *Suggestion:* Always keep this list close by. You definitely need top choices on your cheat sheet!

DAY 13

Say Something Nice to Someone

Joe: You know, Jane, you look like you have really lost some weight.

Jane: Geesh, thanks Joe, I really needed that after this long day!

Joe: We often talk about changing people. Yet, in fact, we know that we can't; however, this is one area where we can truly <u>influence</u> people, so they change.

Jane: Change?

Joe: Yes, say something nice to someone and watch their mood change.

Jane: I guess that's true.

Joe: Think of the power that this gives you.

Jane: Yes, and when you change someone else's mood, in a positive way, it makes you feel good, too, and it is so easy to do. A simple, "How is your day going"; "that blouse really looks good on you"; "you must be in a good mood today, you have a nice glow about you, did you win the lottery?"; "Susan you are really a fast cashier, I love getting in your line!"

Joe: Then you sit back and watch their moods change. Addressing the person by name is a nice touch, Jane. People like to hear their name spoken out loud.

Jane: Sounds so simple, but some days it's just plain hard to do.

Joe: And those are the days when you need to do it the most. Remember the feeling is being returned to you several fold.

Jane: With practice, this becomes second nature and all of a sudden your attitude is seldom in need of adjusting. You simply enjoy helping others feel good.

Joe: Ah ha, without even thinking about it, we have quietly begun to help others. Can you say *empathy*? We will continue to build on this as we move through the days.

Jane: And to think it hasn't even taken any time out of our busy schedule. We simply spoke a kind word.

YOUR PATH: Saying Something Nice does two things: (1) It gives you practice with empathy for others (selflessness); (2) It makes you feel better about yourself, and when you feel better about yourself, you are more likely to stay true to your path.

Don't Be A Cow! Mooing.
Say something nice!

Soulful Enlightenment and Song

Soulful:

"Kind words not only lift our spirits in the moment they are given, but they can linger with us over the years."

- Joseph Wirthlin

Song:

"Beautiful"

- Christina Aguilera

We are all Beautiful!

DAY 13

Say Something Nice to Someone

GAME EXERCISE

Fun game, because it reaps such big rewards with such little effort. Below, write down opportunities to say something nice, and what you might say. To get into the habit, it sometimes help to think about opportunities beforehand.

Suggestions: Trying calling people by their name. For some reason, we all like to hear our names called.

- Have a nice day, John.
- Thank you, Elizabeth.
- I like your hair today, Jane.
- I love that blouse, it really looks good on you, Susan.

Notice how people's moods change by simply saying something nice. This is power.

<u>D A Y 1 4</u>

Give Thanks

Joe: This seems so obvious; I hate to even mention it.

Jane: Yeah, but sometimes it is so obvious we ignore it and take it for granted.

Joe: That is a good point!

Jane: There are also those days where we struggle to think we have anything to be thankful for.

Joe: Yeah, sometimes it feels that the whole world is against us, that we can never catch a break.

Jane: That's exactly right, the "woe is me" I'm going to have a pity party for myself and no one needs to try to stop me.

Joe: Ha-ha, so true.

Jane: This is where Day 5: Practice the Art of Discipline is so important; or Day 8: Be Positive; or Day 9: Squash Negative Thoughts for that matter.

Joe: That's right! See this book does build on itself! In fact, this would be a great discipline activity: Every morning I will rise and write down one thing that I am thankful for.

Jane: Or even better, to help you refocus throughout the day, how about every morning, at lunch and before I go to bed, I will write down one thing I am thankful for?

Joe: For those *really* tough days, it might also be helpful to have a couple pre-written ones you carry with you on the cheat sheet.

Jane: You know what I have on my cheat sheet for "Giving Thanks?"

Joe: There is no telling: Do I want to know?

Jane: The Whos (from Whoville in the *Grinch Who Stole Christmas.*) Think about it. They lost everything, even their food and they still go out and celebrate life itself. That's giving thanks.

Joe: True, and we often say, I wish everyday could be Christmas.

Jane: Yes, and if you strip away all the materialistic part of Christmas there is no reason why we can't have Christmas every day!

Joe: Bingo! I would say that is making our perceptions (expectations) reality.

Jane: Good stuff, Joe.

YOUR PATH: Giving thanks forces us to acknowledge our uniqueness, allowing us to stay true to our path.

Don't Be A Cow!
Give thanks.

Soulful Enlightenment and Song

Soulful:

> "When you rise in the morning, give thanks for the light, for
> your life, for your strength. Give thanks for your food and for the
> joy of living. If you see no reason to give thanks, the fault lies in
> yourself."
>
> > - Tecumseh

Song:

> "Welcome, Christmas (Reprise)"
>
> > - Dr. Seuss: *How the Grinch Stole Christmas* Ensemble

For those who have never seen this movie, The Grinch has stolen
everything from the <u>Whos</u> who come out, join hands and joyfully sing
praises for having each other.

DAY 14

Give Thanks

GAME EXERCISE

Make a list of everything you are thankful for:

Please fill this entire sheet and use additional sheet! *Suggestion:* Keep this handy and look at every time you are having a "not-so-good" day.

DAY 15

The Crown Jewel

That's right. You are the Crown Jewel!

Joe: You are your greatest asset.

Jane: Our <u>quest</u> is at the halfway point and by now we hope you realize just how important you are in this whole process.

Joe: Take the few moments you would spend reading today, to reflect on just how special and important you are to *you*.

YOUR PATH: Only when you recognize and appreciate yourself, can you find and stay true to your path.

Don't Be A Cow! Be you.

Soulful Enlightenment and Song

Soulful:

"You yourself, as much as anybody in the entire universe, deserve your love and affection."

- Buddha

"We cannot think of being acceptable to others until we have first proven acceptable to ourselves."

- Malcolm X

Song:

"Firework"

- Katy Perry

All you have to do is be who you are meant to be and you will light up the world like the fireworks light up the sky on the 4th of July.

<u>D A Y 1 5</u>

The Crown Jewel

GAME EXERCISE

Easy exercise today.

Take a few minutes to stop and reflect on the previous fourteen days. Where have you come? If you feel so compelled, jot down a few notes, comments, phrases on where you think you started and where you are today.

Suggestion: You are the fireworks; you simply need to ignite the spark!

DAY 16

Ask for Forgiveness

Joe: The rising sun and the singing bird, welcoming the start of a new day. Every day starts anew: An opportunity to start over.

Jane: I assume you mean by starting over, starting each day with a clean slate?

Joe: That's right, Jane. And that begins with forgiving ourselves for actions, thoughts or words, spoken that we wished we hadn't.

Jane: Why is it so hard to forgive ourselves, much less ask others to forgive us?

Joe: I believe that some of it stems from the fact we are somewhat embarrassed or not real proud of whatever it is we have done or feel we have done, so we just want to sweep it under the carpet. Pretend as if though it never happened.

Jane: What? Are you saying we squash these events?

Joe: In essence, Yes.

Jane: Therefore, unlike a negative thought that we can squash, this sits inside of us and festers, weighs us down, and wears on our self-confidence.

Joe: That's right. You know sometimes it's even hard to ask God for forgiveness. We just want to ignore it and try to move on.

Jane: Sometimes we think it is hard to forgive others when they do us wrong, but in actuality it is often much harder to forgive ourselves.

Joe: We all have a tendency to be harder on ourselves than we are on others.

Jane: If you think about it, not asking for forgiveness and keeping it bottled up inside is like taking out revenge on ourselves.

Joe: That's brilliant, Jane!

Jane: Wasn't this Jesus's message? That God forgives us if we ask for his forgiveness, which in turn allows us to forgive ourselves so we can go forth and live a productive life?

Joe: When we ask for forgiveness on a regular basis we are admitting that we aren't perfect. Asking for forgiveness forces us to be honest with ourselves. When we do it in prayer or meditation, we are basically confessing to ourselves.

Jane: Your getting a little ahead of yourself. That's tomorrow's lesson.

Joe: Never too early to start learning such an important lesson!

YOUR PATH: It is only when you can start each day fresh, forgiving yourself and others of the mistakes and miscues of yesterday, that you can continually move forward and stay true to your path.

Don't Be A Cow!

Forgive yourself.

Soulful Enlightenment and Song

Soulful:

> "Our father in Heaven, hallowed be your name, your kingdom come, your will be done on Earth as it is in Heaven. Give us today our daily bread. Forgive us our debts, as we also have forgiven our debtors. And lead us not into temptation, but deliver us from the evil."
>
> - The Lord's Prayer

Remember if we expect to be forgiven, we must also forgive.

Song:

> "Why me Lord"
>
> - Kris Kristofferson

This song reminds us that we all make mistakes, and sometimes these mistakes involve following the wrong path for years, but there is always time to stop and find your path, a new beginning, no matter what your past. You can forgive yourself. God's grace is always willing to provide forgiveness.

DAY 16

Ask for Forgiveness

GAME EXERCISE

Writing is strictly optional today: I call this internal confession. During your quiet time (see, Day 6: Take Time For You), think of things you have done that you are not especially proud of. These may even be thoughts. Once you think of them, ask for forgiveness, from yourself, your God, or the person whom these negative thoughts or actions were intended.

Suggestion: Make this a daily habit.

DAY 17

Forgive

Joe: They say, "Never let the sun set on your anger."

Jane: Easier said than done. Because that lady that jumped in front of me at the bakery and grabbed that last chocolate éclair this morning is on the top of my list right now.

Joe: Now, now, Jane. Just yesterday, we discussed admitting that we aren't perfect ourselves. Remember the "forgiveness" thing? We can all be selfish and unpleasant, or should I say not necessarily nice from time to time. Therefore, we can appreciate the fact that other people are as capable of the same.

Jane: So you're saying because we understand ourselves better we become more empathetic towards others?

Joe: That's right, all of a sudden instead of getting angry at the lady who cut you off and got that éclair, you remember that yesterday you did a similar thing to someone else because you were angry at your boss for yelling at you in front of everyone else. Then you theorize that maybe this lady who cut you off for the last chocolate éclair may have been having a bad day and maybe she actually needed it more than you needed it on this day.

Jane: I guess even if we choose not to be cows we all go through this life with similar experiences.

Joe: Although taking the last chocolate éclair is a relatively minor incidence, the same philosophy holds true no matter the consequences of the action.

Jane: I'm not so sure about that. I mean what if someone were to cut off your arm because they were being careless, especially after you had warned them?

Joe: I didn't say it would always be easy. I'm just saying that the same principles hold true. Just think, you are driving, you get distracted and take your eyes off the road for a few seconds, the same action could lead to a minor fender bender or an incident involving a pedestrian. Same action, very different outcomes.

Jane: I guess that's right. We are all careless at times, but I'm not sure I could forgive, if I lost an arm or leg because of someone's carelessness.

Joe: Look at it this way – if you don't ask for forgiveness you become a hostage to yourself. If you don't forgive others, you become a hostage to that person – no matter the consequences.

YOUR PATH: Only when you understand the true nature of forgiveness and forgiving, will you no longer be a hostage to yourself or others and thus will stay true to your path.

Don't Be A Cow!

Or a hostage. Forgive.

Soulful Enlightenment and Song

Soulful:

"A king who wanted to settle accounts with his servant: As he began the settlement, a man who owed him ten thousand talents was brought to him. Since he was not able to pay, the master ordered that he, his wife, his children, and all that he had be sold to repay the debt. The servant fell on his knees before him. "Be patient with me," he begged, "and I will pay back everything." The servant's master took pity on him, canceled the debt and let him go. But, when the servant went out he found one of his fellow servants who owed him a hundred denarii ... His fellow servant fell to his knees and begged him, "Be patient with me," but he refused. Then the mastered called the servant in. "You wicked servant, I canceled all that debt of yours because you begged me to. Shouldn't you have had mercy on your fellow servant just as I had on you?" In anger his master turned him over to the jailers to be tortured, until he should pay back all he owed."

- Mathew 18: 23-34

It is somewhat curious how this works: We seem to want to be forgiven but have a hard time forgiving.

Song:

"Forgiveness"

- Leona Lewis

Although the song is talking about a relationship, the singer admits that they are not perfect; in fact, they admit to being human. Imagine that! We all are, we all make mistakes and no matter the consequences of those mistakes, they are all mistakes. Forgive yourself and others for these mistakes.

DAY 17

Forgive

GAME EXERCISE

Yesterday we examined ourselves for things we needed forgiveness for. Today think of people you could forgive. Possibly, even family or friends with whom you are holding a grudge. If you find it difficult to confront this person, that is okay. Forgive them in your heart. When you have truly forgiven them in your heart, your subsequent actions toward them will let them know. I think that this is sometimes the best way.

DAY 18

Small Acts of Kindness

Jane: Ahhh ... that's so sweet!

Joe: And, oh so simple, if we are prepared for the moment.

Jane: Just think, we already have a head start because on Day 13 we started the process by saying something nice to someone.

Joe: That's right. The problem oftentimes is when we think of being kind or generous, we think in terms of grandeur. We want to do something special; we want to be the super hero that saves the day. Those opportunities may arise for some, but all we really need to do to have a positive impact on others is to perform small acts of kindness.

Jane: That is so true. I remember once, I had a co-worker who had a prolonged injury that kept her at home. I had stopped by the grocery store and bought some pre-made cookie dough, ran home after work, popped it into the oven and brought it over to her house. Nice warm chocolate chip cookies that took all of 30 minutes of my time, but WOW, what a difference it made to this person. She told me once she returned to work, she was convinced that simple act shortened her recovery time by a full week.

Joe: I believe it. It gave her that feeling that she was wanted, needed, appreciated and if not loved at least cared for by a co-worker.

Jane: What is really sad, Joe, is that it made me realize how many opportunities I have had over the years to have the same impact with friends and family, more or less a co-worker.

Joe: Well, I wouldn't be too hard on yourself. We all have missed those opportunities. The key is now that you are conscious of the fact that "Small Acts of Kindness" can reap big rewards you can make it a <u>quest</u> and begin to look for opportunities to perform them. And yes, even a nice word is sometimes all it takes.

YOUR PATH: When we perform "Small Acts of Kindness," we take "Saying Something Nice" to a new level. It will really help you feel better about yourself; thus, not only do you give, but you receive. Receiving this gift will allow you to stay true to your path!

Don't Be A Cow!
Be kind.

Soulful Enlightenment and Song

Soulful:

> "Too often we underestimate the power of a touch, a smile, a
> kind word, a listening ear, an honest compliment, or the smallest
> act of caring, all of which have the potential to turn a life
> around."

> - Leo Buscaglia

Note the significance; not turn someone's day around but turn a life
around! Remember, it's not the big things we do once in a lifetime, but
the daily repeating of small things.

Song:

> "If Everyone Cared"

> - Nickelback

Whenever we show small acts of kindness, we show someone we care.

DAY 18

Small Acts of Kindness

GAME EXERCISE

Write down a few situations in your daily life where you could perform a small act of kindness. The key: think ahead, pre-plan.

- "Let's go out to dinner and take a break from cooking," vs. "Hey you wanna go get somin' to eat?"

- Bring home a goodie from the bakery!

- Pick up special ingredients for a nice dinner.

- Bring a co-worker a deluxe coffee.

- Accept small acts of kindness: If a co-worker brings you a donut, eat and enjoy it. If you started a new diet, exercise an extra 10 minutes instead of saying, "no thanks, I just started a new diet."

DAY 19

Do What You Do Best

Joe: An all too familiar scene!

Jane: What's that?

Joe: Someone trying their best to do something they just aren't good at. Haven't you done that before?

Jane: Well, yes, but sometimes I don't have any reasonable alternative than to suck it up and do it myself.

Joe: We all have those moments, but how many people are stuck in a career doing things they are not particularly good at? Sure they may be able to do them and often do them satisfactory - or even well - but if you asked them they would not consider it one of their strengths.

Jane: How do you suppose that happens?

Joe: Sometimes it is just what we had to do at the time, let's say happenstance.

Jane: And other times?

Joe: For reasons unknown to me, we humans want to overcome our weaknesses by trying to prove to the world that it is not really a weakness at all.

Jane: I guess that make sense. We don't want to expose our weakness because it makes us feel vulnerable, which would be a natural instinct, so we face it head on trying to conquer it.

Joe: Something like that.

Jane: Ok, so how do you propose we know if we are focusing on our weakness as opposed to our strengths?

Joe: Good question! I have the suspicion that it has a lot to do with what we enjoy doing.

Jane: That makes sense as we generally enjoy doing things we are good at!

Joe: Remember when we talked about those days we were doing something we really wanted to do so we bounced out of bed?

Jane: Yes, that would be, Day 8: Be Positive.

Joe: What I have observed is the people who are the happiest at work are those who feel they are doing what they were meant to do. We only have this feeling when we are doing something we are really good at that shows our strengths.

Jane: I guess by doing what you are best at, you will be your best!

Joe: Exactly, that which will make you the happiest!

Jane: And give you the most confidence, I might add.

YOUR PATH: Your strengths are what you are *really* good at and what you really like doing. Uncover your strengths, buried under piles of weaknesses, and you will always be able to stay true to your path.

Don't Be A Cow!

Thrive, doing what you are good at.

Soulful Enlightenment and Song

Soulful:

> "We have different gifts, according to the grace given us. If a man's gift is prophesying, let him use it in proportion to his faith. If it is serving, let him serve; if it is teaching, let him teach; if it is encouraging, let him encourage ... if it is showing mercy, let him do it cheerfully."
>
> - Romans 12:6-8

What is your gift, your talent, your path to share with the world?

Song:

> "Nobody Does It Better"
>
> - Carly Simon

This will be your theme song once you discover "What You Do Best." Why will no one else do it better you might ask? Only you are born with your set of gifts. You and you alone!

DAY 19

Do What You Do Best

GAME EXERCISE

What are your Strengths and Weaknesses? Take your time: Think of work, home, leisure time. Let go of your inhabitations and go for it. What do you really enjoy doing?

Strengths: Weaknesses:

Are you spending more time in the area of your strengths or weaknesses? Discover the fun when you can spend your days doing what you are best at!

Suggestion: Never doubt the possibilities. For Debbi Fields, real enjoyment came from baking, so she started a bakery in the 70's. Today you may be familiar with Mrs. Fields Cookies. Yummy! This is but one of thousands of similar stories.

"What I wanted was to be allowed to do the thing in the world that I did best - which I believed then and believe now is the greatest privilege there is." - Debbi Fields

DAY 20

Remember the Happy Times

Joe: You know Jane, Ingrid Bergman once said, "Happiness is good health and a bad memory."

Jane: Okay, that's a stretch for me. I need a little explanation on that one and what it has to do with today's message.

Joe: Well I assume you have the "good health" part?

Jane: Duh!

Joe: Think about when you are with friends, maybe some of your old high school girl friends. You're out on the town laughing, having a good time. You're happy, right?

Jane: Uh, yes!

Joe: And what are you likely discussing, "the good ole days"?

Jane: Yes, but that doesn't answer my question of how that relates to the quote you started out with, "happiness is a bad memory."

Joe: Ok, what are you and your girlfriends doing? Reminiscing about the fun you had. You have forgotten the horrible hours of studying or bringing home that bad report card (i.e. to be happy you have forgotten all the bad things).

Jane: Oh I get it! The bad memory refers to forgetting the not-so-good times.

Joe: Ah, the light shines in! The key is to remember the happy times when we need them the most.

Jane: Sounds so simple, but when I'm having a bad day, that's almost an impossible task!

Joe: In the movie *Hook,* Tinker Bell tells Peter Pan that if he wants to fly again he needs to remember "his happy place." Peter was desperate to fly so he could save his children from Captain Hook. Once he was able to remember his happy place, he was able to fly.

Jane: Dang, think about the pressure on him to save his kids!

Joe: Absolutely, think of the pressure to make yourself perform. How many of us in times of such pressure would ever take the time to think of our happy memories?

Jane: Maybe we should.

Joe: My point exactly.

YOUR PATH: Don't be a Cow! Bring happy thoughts with you in the most unlikely places and find how they will help you stay true to your path!

Don't Be A Cow!

<u>Seek</u> the happy times.

Soulful Enlightenment and Song

Soulful:

"One of the best ways to make yourself happy in the present is to recall happy times from the past. Photos are a great memory-prompt, and because we tend to take photos of happy occasions, they weight our memories to the good."

- Gretchen Rubin

Gretchen uses photos. Maybe for you, it's jokes, or stories.

Song:

"Happy"

- Pharell

If this little song doesn't bring a smile to your face and make you want to get up and dance well I just don't know what will!

<u>D A Y 2 0</u>

Remember the Happy Times:

GAME EXERCISE

Write down your list of top 10 (or 20) happiest times. Try prioritizing them. It's okay if you have some ties. Once you prepare your final ranking sit back close your eyes and relive these moments. Keep these moments close by to bring cheer when you are having "one of those days." Good to add a couple to cheat sheet.

DAY 21

Learn from the Bad Times

Jane: Hey, I noticed you chose a woman driver. Are you insinuating anything here?

Joe: Remember Day 3: Learn to Laugh? Don't miss the point. It serves as a great lesson to all of us, men and women alike. How many times do we do something that, shall I say, is "somewhat foolish?"

Jane: Okay agreed, we all do things in our life we are not particularly proud of.

Joe: That's right and sometimes it's not even us being foolish, but so-called bad luck. Maybe something bad happened that was not our fault, but had we been really paying attention, we may have avoided the mishap.

Jane: Yeah, like paying attention to the lady cutting me off to get the last chocolate éclair!

Joe: Boy, that really got to you didn't it?

Jane: Yes it did, but I have learned from it. I now pay attention while I'm standing in line. No more texting in line for me.

Joe: You nailed it, Jane! It's all about learning from our mishaps and then moving on! The key is not allowing the event to cause you to think less of yourself.

Jane: Well this particular event did cause there to be less of me, but I understand what you are saying. I learned that I really did need to pay more attention, and by not paying attention, things worse than missing out on the last éclair might happen.

Joe: Exactly.

Jane: Once I learned from my mistake, I lost my anger to the situation, and I actually felt better about myself because I had learned a valuable lesson for the price of 1,000 calories.

Joe: Indeed, when we learn, we are able to move on and actually feel better about ourselves and not worse.

Jane: And the converse is also true: If we don't learn we tend to allow the event to cause us to think less of ourselves. Then we start to form negative images of ourselves.

Joe: That is correct and generally these situations focus on our weaknesses and not our strengths.

Jane: As in my case, I now feel confident watching closely my surroundings and possibly avoiding a purse snatcher versus feeling as though people are always cutting me off, always taking advantage of me, "I'm just pathetic!"

YOUR PATH: Force yourself to learn a lesson from all of life's mishaps, whether they were your fault or not. When you learn, you become more educated and more likely to stay true to your path.

Don't Be A Cow!

Learn from your mistakes.

Soulful Enlightenment and Song

Soulful:

"Without a struggle, there can be no progress."

- Frederick Douglass

Remember as you learn from your mistakes you are progressing on your path to Happiness!

Song:

"Stronger (What doesn't Kill You)"

- Kelly Clarkson

This song reminds us that rough and hard times in our lives make us stronger. When you look at them in this way your can appreciate them because you know when they end you will be a better person.

DAY 21

Learn from the Bad Times

GAME EXERCISE

Write down a few bad times then write down a least one lesson from each.

Okay, it's done.

You are progressing. Now, move on!

<u>D A Y   2 2</u>

Forget the Awful Times

Joe: Today's lesson is going to be very short.

Jane: Well, I think after 21 grueling days everyone could use that.

Joe: Today we have gone from bad times to awful times.

Jane: Yeah, I've had of few of those myself.

Joe: Sometimes these awful times are just that. For some reason, we all experience them and we all have to work through them.

Jane: Yeah, sometimes it feels that we go through these times to make us tougher, to test our strength and resolve.

Joe: Yes, and as a final word: Often times you will hear football coaches say after a slaughter-fest defeat, "this was so bad and doesn't reflect who we are as a team. We will just throw this film away. We can't gain anything useful from this disaster!"

Jane: Yeah, I suppose we just have to acknowledge that these things happen and move on.

Joe: Correct, and that's what we are going to do. MOVE ON!

YOUR PATH: When you can put the awful times behind you, you will be able to stay true to your path.

Don't Be A Cow!

Mooove on.

Be <u>extraordinary</u>.

Soulful Enlightenment and Song

Soulful:

> "As rain makes its way into a badly roofed house, so passion makes its way into an unreflecting mind.
>
> As rain does not make its way into a well-roofed house, so passion does not make its way into a reflecting mind."
>
> - The Dhamapada (Scriptures) Sayings of the Buddha.

It is the unreflecting mind, the one that can forget the awful times, that is full of passion!

Song:

> "Let It Go," the movie, *Frozen*
>
> - Idina Menzel

This is an upbeat reminder of such a simple message: "Let it go," the past is now behind you, if you allow it to be.

DAY 22

Forget the Awful Times

GAME EXERCISE

Since we are asking you to forget the awful times, it would make no sense to ask you to write them down. We, for real, want you to forget them. Stuff happens. Now, let's move on to Day 23.

D A Y   2 3

Ask Not What Others Can Do for You

Ask What You Can Do for Others

Joe: How this would be a different world if we all awakened each day and recited these words, then went forth and performed them!

Jane: Absolutely. No matter what you thought of President Kennedy, these are certainly good words to live by. But, isn't it sort of like "Small Acts of Kindness"?

Joe: Not really. I mean obviously doing something for someone else is certainly an act of kindness; however, this is not only an act of generosity, it is a philosophy of life. It says forget the self-righteous pity party and use your God-given talent to help others.

Jane: When you say philosophy of life, are you saying that this is more about a mind set and not actually doing?

Joe: Yes and no!

Jane: Oh, I just love when you start in on the Yeses and Nos.

Joe: Hold on, bear with me – Yes, in the fact that it begins with an attitude and then culminates in doing. It's certainly not enough to think about helping others, but all actions begin with a thought.

Jane: So you mean it signifies how we approach life?

Joe: Bingo. In other words, we put the needs of others before the needs of our self.

Jane: Seek to help others!

YOUR PATH: In today's "Me" society, when you put the needs of others before yours, you will truly be on a unique path thus allowing you to stay true to your path.

Selfishness = Cowism

Don't Be A Cow!

Soulful Enlightenment and Song

Soulful:

> "I was hungry and you gave me food, I was thirsty and you gave me drink, I was a stranger and you welcomed me, I was naked and you clothed me, I was sick and you visited me, I was in prison and you came to me ...Truly, I say to you, as you did it to one of the least of these my brethren, you did it to me."
>
> - Mathew 25: 35-40.

Live your life to help others no matter who they may be.

Song:

> "America the Beautiful"
>
> - Ray Charles

Whether you are an American, Russian, German or some other nationality, it is always nice to feel a part of something bigger than yourself (just don't forget to be yourself). We accomplish this by having the attitude of serving others.

DAY 23

Ask Not What Others Can Do for You,

Ask What You Can Do for Others

GAME EXERCISE

This can be a tough one because it requires action on your part. Below write down some ideas you have where you can help others. *Hint:* Think small and build into grandeur. Remember, if you find this difficult because of a busy schedule or if it's totally new to you, the first step is writing down a few ideas, then as you go through the day, look for other opportunities. It's okay, if it takes you a little while to move into action, but it is important that you start thinking about it right away.

This may be as simple as taking the time to listen to someone.

DAY 24

Practice Makes Perfect;
Practice Happiness

Joe: You know what is so great about today's lesson, Jane?

Jane: What's that?

Joe: Society gives us plenty of opportunities to practice.

Jane: Amen to that. You wake up, you feel good, you eat a good breakfast, your humming a favorite tune and then *BAM!* You have to go out the front door and enter the world. Drivers being crazy, co-workers being critical, bosses trying to meet deadlines, and it goes on and on and on!

Joe: Ha-ha! Sounds like you're talking from experience, Jane.

Jane: And am I!

Joe: That is the truly great thing about this – the opportunities for practice are endless. The key is to look at it that way, merely a test to see how you are doing.

Jane: Well, good thing there are plenty of tests because I'm going to need a bunch to average out to a "C." I assure you, I fail much more than I pass.

Joe: You can't look at it that way, Jane. It's only failing if you refuse to acknowledge the bad (negative) responses and don't think how you could have responded differently. Remember, you can only control your response, not others actions or other external stimuli.

Jane: Let me see if I have this right: If we practice our response to others actions, eventually we will actually have a perfect response.

Joe: Dang. You are really starting to get the hang of this stuff.

Jane: Well our goal from the outset of this book is to achieve happiness everyday.

Joe: That's right, achieving happiness on your own terms and not society's: Don't Be A Cow!

YOUR PATH: Practice, Practice, and Practice: The only way you will stay true to your path.

Don't Be A Cow!

Accept all that society throws at you as practice. Practice to be a better you.

Soulful Enlightenment and Song

Soulful:

> "The more you bring your choices into the level of your conscious awareness, the more you will make those choices which are spontaneously correct - both for you and those around you.

> "When you feel frustrated or upset by a person or a situation, remember that you are not reacting to the person or situation. These are your feelings."

> - Deepak Chopra

Song:

> "Happiest Girl in the Whole USA"

> - Donna Fargo

An oldie that many have probably never heard, but what a nice, cheerful, fun and simple song.

DAY 24

Practice Happiness

GAME EXERCISE

Jot down a couple of times when someone said something that upset you or that made you mad.

Think how you could have practiced happiness and not let a comment (or comments) move you off your path.

Now, jot down a couple of times when circumstances didn't go your way. Maybe a rainy day when you had planned a picnic or a flat tire on the way to the airport.

How could you have used the occasion to practice "Happiness"?

DAY 25

Try Something New

Joe: Hey Jane, I have a question for ya!

Jane: Ok, shoot! You know me. I'll have an answer.

Joe: Let me introduce my "second squash theory." How do you know you don't like squash if you have never had squash?

Jane: Really, Joe?

Joe: Hold on – hang with me on this: As we get older our taste buds change, correct?

Jane: Yes, I like things now I didn't when I was a kid.

Joe: Ah ha! How do you know that?

Jane: Well, I tried them again as an adult.

Joe: My point exactly, you tried them again or you tried something new.

Jane: Yes, I guess that's right.

Joe: Just like our taste buds, we ourselves change because of our daily life experiences.

Jane: So things I might not have liked doing as a kid I might like today?

Joe: Yes, in fact this book is a perfect example. When I was in school, I would never have written a book.

Jane: It's about trying things with an open mind and trying new things.

Joe: As we go through life, we all have a tendency to get caught in ruts, those day-to-day routines. After awhile, we are bound to these routines. These routines are not just our schedules but what we eat, the people we socialize with, the stores we frequent, even what we do in our spare time. For most of us, these things probably vary little.

Jane: Well I guess when you put it like that, it does make things seem kind of boring.

Joe: I don't know that boring is the right word, but it is a lifestyle that is not conducive to exploring new adventures. And, new adventures may simply be discovering what it is you really "want to" do.

Jane: Yes, but I think you are walking on thin ice here. I know people who are very routine-oriented and would totally come unglued if they tried to change that.

Joe: I'm not saying it's about changing your entire lifestyle and all your routines. Remember routine is more than your daily schedule.

Simply start trying something different. Make sure you see today's game exercise; this can really be fun!

Jane: When we try new things, we are subject to find all kinds of treasures.

Joe: Exactly. If you are currently not finding treasures in your life, maybe you should start looking in different places.

Jane: It certainly can add freshness to your life, should I say, a little <u>zest!</u>

YOUR PATH: Your gift to the world may be hiding in the most unlikely of places; <u>seeking</u> new things will always help you stay true to your path.

Don't Be A Cow!

Try something new today.

Soulful Enlightenment and Song

Soulful:

"When he was forty years old, it came into his heart to visit his brethren, the sons of Israel."

- Acts 7:23

This is Paul referring to Moses. Look at the plush life Moses had, then at age 40, he tried some "squash" and liked it. Then he found his path. And, man what a path he blazed. It's never too late!

Song:

"I Hope You Dance"

- Lee Ann Womack

A song about <u>seeking</u> opportunity, living life to its fullest. Opportunity comes to those who look in new places!

<u>DAY 25</u>

Try Something New

GAME EXERCISE

Start small:

- Try a fruit or vegetable you've never had.

- Go to a different restaurant or try a new item at your favorite one.

- Drive a different way to work.

- Have Fun! Feel the Excitement of simply trying something new!

Note your "Something New":

Who knows, before long you may even try a new job, a new career, (one at which you are best at), or a new friend!

DAY 26

Believe What You Believe

Jane: Boy does that picture say 1,000 words!

Joe: Yes, it does!

Jane: We hear and read so much today, how would anybody even know what is true and what is not true?

Joe: Well, what do you believe? Do you even know any more?

Jane: That's what I'm saying; I don't even know any more!

Joe: I propose to you that you *do* know you just don't take the time to think about it. Then if what you believe goes against the consensus of the group you tend to go back into *cow* mode (fall in line with everyone else!).

Jane: Isn't that the truth. Just last week, I went out with my usual lunch crowd and they were all on the latest diet kick. All the way to the restaurant they were talking about how great it was and how everyone was doing it. Man was I looking forward to that big ole bacon cheeseburger and fries, but as you can guess, I played the "cow" and ordered a salad. I agree that eating a salad is good for you, but I had been eating salads all week trying to get off those few extra pounds, which I did, so I was ready to celebrate a little.

Joe: A classic story, Jane. A similar thing happened to me involving a bike ride with the boys at the office. Couldn't walk for a week! Like you, I believe that it's good to exercise, but not necessarily kill yourself in the process. I'm certainly not into "no pain, no gain" anymore!

Jane: I guess you are right, deep down we all sort of know what we believe … sometimes we just hold it in, so people don't think we're weird!

Joe: The problem is I don't know if we do know what we believe any more. It requires us to sift through all the information and think for ourselves.

Jane: Think for ourselves: What an idea! Even though we are using diet, exercise and current events of the day as examples, it's a process when you stop thinking for yourself. It sneaks up on you. Think about your career, your social circles …

YOUR PATH: When you believe what you believe and can share it comfortably with others, you will instill confidence in yourself and be able to stay true to your path!

Don't Be A Cow!
Think for yourself and don't be ashamed to share it with others!

Soulful Enlightenment and Song

Soulful:

"He said, 'Come,' so Peter got out of the boat and walked on the water and came to Jesus; but when he saw the wind, he was afraid, and beginning to sink he cried out, 'Lord, save me.' Jesus immediately reached out his hand and caught him, saying to him, 'O man of little faith, why did you doubt?'"

- Mathew 14:29-31

As long as Peter believed he could walk on water, he could, but an external force (wind) came along and made him doubt his own belief, and once doubt entered, he sunk. External forces can be from nature or from man! Remember, when you believe without doubt, you can walk on water!

Song:

"Believe in Yourself"

- Diana Ross

DAY 26

Believe What You Believe

GAME EXERCISE

In today's society, we are inundated with information. With all this information, we often forget to think for ourselves.

Trying to block out all the external noises, write down what it is you believe: Diet, exercise, religion (faith), daily routines, child raising, etc.

DAY 27

Dream

Joe: You know, Jane, some people say "no" to dreaming!

Jane: Yeah, I know, right? How boring!

Joe: They say that if you don't write your dreams down you are just wasting thought! They say dreaming is simply goals never written down, thus they are never achieved.

Jane: Like you're just living some sort of Disney fairy tale!

Joe: Well I say it's all balderdash! We go through life hearing all kinds of stories about people realizing their dreams. When it is near and dear to your heart, why must you write it down - lest you forget?

Jane: Yeah, really. I've sort of looked at dreaming as my brain at recess. It is free to play and run around and concoct any kind of images and scenarios my imagination can come up with.

Joe: That's a good way of putting it, though, I must say, I never thought of it that way.

Jane: I mean we have our dreams that we hope may somehow come true, like our knight in shining armor coming to sweep us off our feet. I used to dream about it all the time when I was a girl. When I dreamt about Mr. Right, I didn't even cut corners. My Mr. Right was right! And, now I wake every morning with one constant in my life - I made one right decision! All because of a dream!

Joe: That's an interesting point about dreaming - we don't allow ourselves to cut corners. We think of ourselves in a positive light, always full of confidence and sure of ourselves, and always envisioning positive situations and outcomes.

Jane: Absolutely! Now, eventually you have to come out of these dreams and live life, of course, but I think dreams can be a great stepping-stone in helping us obtain what it is we want out of life. Like on Day 11: Visualize, dreaming is actually practicing visualizing.

Joe: That is so true. The reason more of us don't "realize our dreams" is because we can't lose our inhibitions, those negative voices inside our heads that say we can't!

Jane: There is a common sarcastic saying today, "I'm living the dream." Now, remove the sarcasm: "Don't Be A Cow" and "Just do it"!

YOUR PATH: Learn to dream without inhibitions, and you will always stay true to your path!

Dream on.
Don't Be A Cow! Just do it.

Soulful Enlightenment and Song

Soulful:

> "Our dreams are first-hand creations, rather than residues of waking life. We have the capacity or infinite creativity; at least while dreaming, we partake of the power of the Spirit, the infinite Godhead that creates the cosmos."
>
> - Jackie Gleason

Dream and connect to your spirit - Connect to You!

Song:

> "Dream On!"
>
> - Aerosmith

A little heavy rock but it has all of the necessary elements for a good song - Upbeat, positive and simple. When we lose the negative inhabitations, our dreams will come true. Dream on!

DAY 27

Dream

GAME EXERCISE

Do not write them down.

Today we are just going to dream.

Dream big, then begin to live your dream!

<u>D A Y 2 8</u>

Attitude, Attitude, Attitude

Pessimist - Complains about Wind.

Optimist - Waits for wind to Change.

Leader - Adjusts the sails.

Jane: Joe, isn't this sort of saying the same thing as Day 4: Want To and Day 8: Positive?

Joe: It's the ole "yes" and "no" thing, Jane!

Jane: Great, I should have never asked!

Joe: "Want to" and being "Positive" are both attitudes, but they center on a certain drive. Attitude centers around your overall view of life.

Jane: I can agree with that. And, because this book is about being happy, we want happy attitudes?

Joe: Yes, but there is more – Attitude involves more than being positive and having "want to" to make it through everyday life. As we know, there are just days when being positive is almost impossible. Not only is our mood foul, it seems as though the whole world is against us. We can't dream because we are trapped in this awful thing that we don't even know what it is. We will just call it an ill mood.

Jane: I've had just a few of those days over the years!

Joe: Sadly for some these moods can last much longer than a day or two.

Jane: It's not hard to fall into that situation.

Joe: So even though we may not be able to force ourselves to be positive and we may not have a whole lot of "want to," we must always understand that our attitude is strictly ours to control, and we must not give that control to anyone else.

Jane: Even though we are mad at the world, and nothing is going right, we still have the ability to control our attitude ... whether we choose to or not.

Joe: And remember, it's not expected to change us to a positive attitude immediately, but to simply keep reminding ourselves that we have the ability to change our mood and our disposition.

Jane: I guess by continually reminding ourselves that we can change our attitude makes us feel like we are in control.

Joe: Yes, and when we feel in control we are much more likely to change to a positive place much faster.

Jane: I understand the picture now, Joe! Both the optimist and the pessimist are waiting for an external force to change things whereas the leader relies on his own self.

Joe: You said it all, Jane!

YOUR PATH: To find your path you must be a leader, a leader of one! When you understand this, you will be able to stay true to your path!

Don't Be A Cow!

Your attitude is yours and yours alone.

Never let others try to control it.

Soulful Enlightenment and Song

Soulful:

> "Nothing can stop the man with the right mental attitude from achieving his goal; nothing on earth can help the man with the wrong mental attitude."
>
> - Thomas Jefferson

Be sure you have the right attitude!

Song:

> "Changes in Latitudes, Changes in Attitudes"
>
> - Jimmy Buffet

DAY 28

Attitude, Attitude, Attitude

GAME EXERCISE

Life is full of choices: e.g. study hard/goof off; go to college/go to work; get married/stay single; have children/don't have children. Jot down a couple of these choices that stick out in your life:

At the time you made these choices did you recognize them as choices or were they just the "next steps in life"?

When the paths we choose are simply "next steps," we fall into the optimist/pessimist role. When we consciously choose our path, we play the role of a leader, a leader of one. When you are leading *you*, you will always have the Attitude, Attitude, Attitude.

Control What You Can Control

Jane: Yesterday you were just talking about control as in controlling your attitude, what's going to be different today?

Joe: You are correct in that attitude does play a big role today.

Jane: See, I knew I was on to something!

Joe: Yesterday we spoke of using our attitude to control ourselves and to not allow others to control us, but what about when we try to control others?

Jane: You mean the girl in the picture?

Joe: Exactly. How do you think that is going to work out? We all know that we hate when others try to control us, so why do we try to control others?

Jane: Because it makes us feel powerful?

Joe: Maybe for some, but I think that the real reason is our Cow Theory playing out in reverse.

Jane: Wow, I'm really lost now.

Joe: It's not that complicated. Think about us following others because we want to feel a part of the group. We don't want to be different because it's uncomfortable.

Jane: Okay, so far so good!

Joe: Well, then doesn't it stand to reason that by controlling others we are asking them to follow us, to agree with us?

Jane: I see, so we are still being a cow, we just happen to be the lead cow?

Joe: Exactly! You see, Jane, we must not only choose our path, we must encourage others to do the same. We must use our experiences and knowledge to influence others, but not to control others. When we try to control others, we are simply using others to validate our own beliefs.

Jane: Oh wow, I see that now! Joe, this has really turned on some lights for me, but why wait until Day 29? I mean we are almost at the end!

Joe: Without Days 1 – 28, the lights you saw turn on would have never turned on. Before you stop trying to control others, you must first believe in yourself without validation from others. Controlling others and others controlling you is cowism in a nutshell. Without cracking that nut, you will struggle to find happiness. You must understand that you have a specific purpose in this life and so does everyone else. Find yours and <u>influence</u> others to find theirs.

Jane: That's really neat and here at the end it sort of pulls everything together.

YOUR PATH: Imagine ... if everyone found their own unique gift and shared it with a friend we would discover that each of us could stay true to our paths!

Don't Be A Cow!

Then you can <u>influence</u> others.

Soulful Enlightenment and Song

Soulful:

"To be at peace in any endeavor, we must release our need to control the outcome."

- Diane Dreher (from *The Tao of Inner Peace*)

As you move through life, replace controlling thoughts with influencing thoughts and feel the happiness within!

Song:

"Lean on Me"
– Bill Withers

This song reminds us that we all need friends. We just need our friends to help and support us and not control us. And, we need to do likewise!

DAY 29

Control What You Can Control

GAME EXERCISE

Write down a few times where you have tried to control someone or a particular outcome. How important was controlling this person or situation to you staying true to your path? Now how could you have achieved the same thing using <u>influence</u>?

<u>D A Y   3 0</u>

Never Stop

Joe: Jane, we have finally reached the end!

Jane: Not quite, don't we have one more day after today?

Joe: Technically speaking we do, but I sort of look at tomorrow as dessert. One last tidbit of information, something to reflect upon and an introduction to our next writing <u>adventure</u>!

Jane: Okay enough about tomorrow's dessert. What kind of meat and potatoes do you have for us today?

Joe: We have all heard of the famous quotes from various famous people who have in essence said, "Never, ever quit!" I want to express it a little differently...

Jane: Imagine that!

Joe: Get comfortable, grab hold of the steering wheel and choose your direction! No matter how many destinations you reach, the road is never going to stop. What a _quest_!

YOUR PATH: In the end, there is one path, which is yours. When you never stop <u>seeking</u> it, not only will you find your path, but you will always stay true to your path!

Don't Be A Cow!

Persevere and find <u>adventure</u> everyday.

Soulful Enlightenment and Song

Soulful:

> " By perseverance the snail reached the ark."
>
> - Charles Spurgeon

What an image, keep it in your head and recall it every time you are in a <u>challenging</u> situation and are ready to give up.

Song:

> "The Climb"
>
> – Miley Cyrus

An upbeat, feel good song that reminds us of that age-old adage, "it is the journey, not the destination." Approach your journey with perseverance accept the bad with the good and no matter what you do …

Don't Be A Cow!

D A Y 3 0

Never Stop

GAME EXERCISE

Look back to Day 27: Dream. It's blank, remember? That's because you were dreaming! Write that dream below. Underneath write the phrase, "Today, this is my mountain and I'm never going to stop the climb!"

D A Y 3 1

Return to Where You Started

"We shall not cease from exploration,
and the end of all our exploring
will be to arrive where we started
and know the place for the first time."
- T.S. Eliot

Jane: Okay, what are you saying here? That it's time to start back over at Day 1?

Joe: Not at all! Let me explain: Have you ever noticed something new, while driving a route that you drive every day and wondered how long it's been there? Or, have you ever learned a new word and then all of a sudden you hear that word being used everywhere?

Jane: Yes…

Joe: The principles in this book are like that. In fact, all of life is that way. Several months after reading this book you will flip through it and some of the words will say something different. Or, you will be listening to the playlist and a song will move you differently. Even though you have been on this journey, you will discover new aspects for the first time.

Jane: Why is that?

Joe: You see, life is a circle and we, as humans, want to make everything a straight line. That is, a line with a definite beginning and a definite end, but in actuality it is just the opposite.

Jane: A straight line as in, "today is my first day of work, I will be able to retire 25 years from today!"

Joe: That's it! Work simply occupies part of the circle and today you really don't have any idea how much of that circle will be occupied by work. So why be concerned with it? Because life is a circle, we keep coming back around to the same places, and because our life experiences change with every pass, we see the same things, but we see them differently. Thus, we are even able to see work differently!

Jane: And, because it's a circle, and we're constantly trying to make it a straight line, we are constantly working against the natural system.

Joe: Exactly! When we live our lives as straight lines, we live in terms of constant beginnings and ends, and not in continuums. When we wake each morning, we are somewhere on our line as opposed to living each day for itself and the experiences that the day has to offer.

Jane: We sort of short-change ourselves! I see that now.

Joe: We must understand that we can totally change our lives by looking at the same things, yet seeing them differently.

YOUR PATH: Life is paved with experiences from each day, don't short change yourself; accepting these experiences will enable you to stay true to your path.

Don't Be A Cow!

Live your circle of life
gaining experiences from each day.

Make beginnings and ends
a distant memory.

Soulful Enlightenment and Song

Soulful:

"Everything's a circle. We're each responsible for our own actions. It will come back."

- Betty Laverdure Ojibway

Song:

" Circle of Life," the film, *The Lion King*

– Lebo M, performed by Carmen Twillie

All life travels in circles, jump on yours and live.

DAY 31

Return to Where You Started

GAME EXERCISE

Write down the five days that meant the most to you:

1.

2.

3.

4.

5.

As you revisit this book notice if these five days have changed. If so note the ones that change.

Below, draw a circle. Inside the circle, write your name.

This is your Circle of Life. Pick a spot on the circle where you want to jump in and leap!

Epilogue

Joe and Jane sincerely hope that you have enjoyed this <u>adventure</u>.

Believe us when we say, we have lived this book and not just written it. We have experienced the ups and downs of everyday life. From the good times, great times and horrible times, and all points in-between; from good health to bad health, good financial times to down-to-our-last dime financial times, we have lived each day.

And through it all, we have been able to find happiness. Hopefully, this book shares what we found helpful, and by referring to it daily, you find purpose, fulfillment and happiness!

A final song:

> "Family Tradition"
>
> > - Hank Williams Jr.

In this song, Hank describes living out the songs that he has written.

***

Joe & Jane:

> This song sums up our experience in putting this book together. We had to live each day to prove it to be true - very exhausting ... Nonetheless, very rewarding! We hope that you find it as helpful as we have in <u>seeking</u> purpose, fulfillment and happiness. And, please, don't forget ...

"Don't Be A Cow!"

We invite you to share songs and quotes you have found helpful on your journey toward happiness on our website, DontBeACow.com.

Appendix

DON'T BE A COW! PLAY LIST

Day	Song
Prologue	"Life is a Highway" - Rascal Flatts
1. Be Who You Are!	"Stand in the Light" - Jordan Smith; "Try" - Colbie Caillat
2. Learn to Smile	"Smile" - Nat King Cole
3. Learn to Laugh	"The Mississippi Squirrel" - Ray Stevens
4. "Want to"	"Don't Stop Believin'" - Journey
5. Discipline	"Gonna Fly Now," Theme from *Rocky* - Bill Conti
6. Take Time for You	"Lord is it Mine" – SuperTramp; "In My Room" - Beach Boys
7. Nature	"What a Wonderful World" - Louis Armstrong
8. Be Positive	"The Devil Went Down to Georgia" - Charlie Daniels
9. Squash Negative Thoughts	"X's and O's" - Elle King
10. What Do You Want?	"You Can't Always Get What You Want" – Rolling Stones
11. Visualize	"Paint Me a Birmingham" - Tracy Lawrence
12. Revisit #3	"Mr. Mom" - Lonestar
13. Say Something Nice	"Beautiful" - Christina Aguilera
14. Give Thanks	"Welcome Christmas" - Dr. Seuss, *How the Grinch Stole Christmas* Ensemble
15. The Crown Jewel	"Firework" - Katy Perry

16. Ask for Forgiveness	"Why Me Lord?" - Kris Kristofferson
17. Forgive	"Forgiveness" - Leona Lewis
18. Small Acts of Kindness	"If Everyone Cared" - Nickleback
19. Do What You Do Best	"Nobody Does It Better" - Carly Simon
20. Remember the Happy Times	"Happy" - Pharell
21. Learn from the Bad Times	"Stronger" - Kelly Clarkson
22. Forget the Awful Times	"Let It Go," *Frozen* - Idina Menzel
23. Ask Not What Others Can Do for You	"America, the Beautiful" – Ray Charles
24. Practice Happiness	"Happiest Girl in the Whole USA" - Donna Fargo
25. Try Something New	"I Hope You Dance" - Lee Ann Womack
26. Believe What You Believe	"Believe in Yourself" - Diana Ross
27. Dream	"Dream On" - Aerosmith
28. Attitude, Attitude, Attitude	"Changes in Latitudes, Changes in Attitudes" - Jimmy Buffett
29. Control	"Lean On Me" - Bill Withers
30. Never Stop	"The Climb" - Miley Cyrus
31. Return to Where You Started	"Circle of Life," *The Lion King* – Lebo M/Carmen Twillie
Epilogue	Family Tradition - Hank Williams Jr.

YOUR PLAY LIST

Day	Song
Prologue	
1. Be Who You Are!	
2. Learn to Smile	
3. Learn to Laugh	
4. "Want to"	
5. Discipline	
6. Take Time for You	
7. Nature	
8. Be Positive	
9. Squash Negative Thoughts	
10. What Do You Want?	

11. Visualize	
12. Revisit #3	
13. Say Something Nice	
14. Give Thanks	
15. The Crown Jewel	
16. Ask For Forgiveness	
17. Forgive	
18. Small Acts of Kindness	
19. Do What You Do Best	
20. Remember the Happy Times	
21. Learn From the Bad Times	
22. Forget the Awful Times	
23. Ask Not What Others Can Do for You	
24. Practice Happiness	

25. Try Something New	
26. Believe What You Believe	
27. Dream	
28. Attitude, Attitude, Attitude	
29. Control What You Can Control	
30. Never Stop	
31. Return to Where You Started	
Epilogue	

Who They Are

Day	Author	Who They Are
1	Alfred Korzybski (1879-1950)	Polish- American scholar. Developed field of Semantics
Prologue	Berthold Auerbach (1812-1882)	German-Jewish poet
31	Betty Laverdure Ojibway (1930-2014)	Indian woman, Lawyer and Indian activist. "Cherished the value of integrity … facing adversity with humor"
15, 22	Buddha (563 BCE)	Ascetic and sage on whose teaching Buddhism was founded
30	Charles Spurgeon (1834-1892)	British Particular Baptist preacher
Prologue	Dalai Lama (1935 -)	Monk of the Gelug school of Tibetan Buddhism
24	Deepak Chopra (1947-)	Indian-American author; promoter of alternative medicine
29	Diane Dreher (1946 -)	American author, *The Tao of Inner Peace*
3	Ethel Barrymore (1879-1959)	American actress, "First Lady of American Theater"
21	Frederick Douglas (1818-1895)	African-American social reformer, orator and author
20	Gretchen Rubin (1966 -)	American author, blogger and speaker
20	Ingrid Bergman (1915-1982)	Swedish actress
11	Jack Nicklaus (1940 -)	Professional golfer
27	Jackie Gleason (1916-1987)	American comedian; actor

12	Jimmy Buffet (1946 -)	American musician; songwriter
13	Joseph Wirthlin (1917-2008)	American businessman; religious leader
4, 7	Kahlil Gibran (1883-1931)	Lebanese-American artist, poet and writer
18	Leo Buscaglia (1924-1998)	American author; professor of Special Education, USC
7	Luther Standing Bear (1868-1939)	Native American author, educator and philosopher
3	Mahatma Gandhi (1869-1948)	Hindu Leader of the Indian Independence movement in British-ruled India; assassinated
15	Malcolm X (1925-1965)	African-American Muslim minister and activist; assassinated
6	Nelson Mandela (1918-2013)	South African anti-apartheid revolutionary, politician and philanthropist; President of South Africa, 1994 to 1999
11	Nick Faldo (1957-)	Professional golfer, TV commentator
1	Robert Frost (1874-1963)	American poet
2	Mother Teresa (1910-1997)	Albanian-Indian Roman Catholic nun and missionary
	Socrates (399 BC)	Greek philosopher
Prolog	Samuel Jackson (1948-)	American actor and film producer
9	Robert Schuller (1926-1915)	American Christian evangelist
14	Tecumseh (1768-1813)	Native American leader of the Shawnee; sided with Britain in War of 1812; Killed in Battle of Thames

28	Thomas Jefferson (1743-1826)	American founding father and the principal author of the Declaration of Independence; 3rd U.S. President
31	TS Eliot (1888-1965)	British poet, playwright and publisher, born in the U.S.A.
5	William Feather (1889-1981)	American publisher and author
Various	Holy Bible	Revised Standard Version & New International Version

Cheat Sheet

GAME EXERCISE

Write highlights or meaningful entries from individual daily game exercises. You may want to tear this page out and carry with you to gain its full effects!

Acknowledgements

We would like to thank Chanin Brown, Dorothy McDaniel, Candice Wayman, and Stan Veraart for their support and honest feedback in the early days and Angie Harper for giving us the idea, many moons ago!

We would also like to thank Pat Achilles for her great illustrations that made our words come to life. And, Gary James for going well beyond contractual obligations and handling details that we never even knew existed and doing it all with a great sense of humor. A must working with us! Gary has truly made this book become a reality.

Last, but certainly not least, we would also like to dedicate this book to Mother Nature, which supplies us professionally and provides us a great playground. For this we will give back, through our non-profit Land and Trees Unlimited, a large percentage of the proceeds of this book.

The Authors

George and Rachel Barker have been married since 2006. They both brought two children from previous marriages into the family. Rachel has a degree in Landscape and Ornamental Horticulture. George has a degree in Forest Resource and Conservation. Thus, they share a passion for trees and the great out of doors.

This book is their first writing endeavor and has truly been a labor of love.

Made in the USA
San Bernardino, CA
22 January 2017